Christianity in a collapsing culture

O. R. Johnston
(Director, Nationwide Festival of Light)

Exeter
The Paternoster Press

ISBN: 0 85364 200 1

The substance of this paper was first delivered as
a lecture to the annual Leicester Conference of
Evangelical ministers in April 1975. The conference brings together pastors and clergy who
affirm the biblical theology of the Reformation.

Australia:
Emu Book Agencies Pty., Ltd.,
63 Berry Street, Granville, N.S.W. 2142

South Africa:
Oxford University Press,
P.O. Box 1141, Oxford House,
11 Buitencingle St., Cape Town

Made and printed in Great Britain for
The Paternoster Press Paternoster House
3 Mount Radford Crescent Exeter Devon
by Maslands (Tiverton) Ltd. Devon

Introduction

Britain today stands on the brink of a precipice. Many have watched with concern the changes in the mood of the nation over the last twenty years. War-weary and unable to glimpse a new moral imperative to replace the one task which we knew to be right and good—the destruction of the evils of Nazi Germany; racked by a nagging sense of lost identity since the dissolution of the Empire at the very time when communist imperialism was spreading its tentacles so successfully around the whole globe; confused by the influx of people of different racial groups and cultures from other continents, and forced to attempt a pluralist synthesis of a magnitude unknown and even unimagined in British history; economically weakened by the oil prices dictated by the pressures of an Arab nationalism united as never before. . . . Britain has been the prey of forces which have weakened and blurred any sense of strong common purpose.

Yet deeper than all these factors has been the decline of shared moral and spiritual convictions. In an age when the churches looked inward, muddled and powerless, we saw the emergence of a new generation of mass-communicators in magazines, newspapers, radio and TV, a group of young professionals unshaped by any conviction of the greatness of Britain's past— intelligent, pragmatic, cynically humorous, historically ignorant and spiritually shallow, uncommitted save to constant innovation and to the refusal to take anything too seriously. Their attitude spread from theatre to theology, a self-consciously radical posture became obligatory, so that what were previously considered humane conventions were ridiculed as repressive taboos.

To add to these difficulties, economic self-restraint went overboard in the 1970s as moral restraint had been jettisoned in the 1960s. In a mindless leap-frogging progression of wage claims, various groups of organised industrial workers pressed for ever higher wages, and compliant governments printed more money and incurred vast foreign debts to placate them. The professions—doctors, teachers and nurses—engaged in "industrial action"—i.e. strikes—for the first time in their long history. The ethic of public service seemed to have been extinguished. Increasingly now observers of all shades of opinion see Britain as on the point of collapse—culturally, politically, economically and morally. What is our Christian duty in this situation?

These pages outline a Christian theology of cultural involvement. They articulate a concern which the writer believes to be faithful to Holy Scripture. It is his unashamed conviction that

> God's Word for all their craft and force
> One moment will not linger,
> But spite of hell shall have its course;
> 'Tis written by His finger.

I offer an evangelical analysis of Christian responsibility. It may say little that is new to some readers, for its theme has been that of many Christian thinkers from Augustine of Hippo to Francis Schaeffer. Yet other believers may find the topic new and even thrilling, for biblical truth has a way of coming alive in a new way as fresh situations confront the church in the challenges of a new social setting. Younger Christians with little background knowledge of history, theology or cultural perspective may well find this re-statement of principles a help to their Christian testimony in times of change and decay.

Content and Context

At the very deepest level Christian testimony in any age is always the same. Take the first chapter of John's First Epistle. Christian testimony asserts the facts that God is Light and that no man can say he is not a sinner; that the eternal Word of Life was with the Father from all eternity yet has become incarnate; that through the blood of Jesus Christ men and women can now be cleansed from all sin, since God is faithful and just to forgive us our sins, and that when he forgives us we begin to enjoy fellowship with him, with his Son and with each other, and we experience great joy. These things are part of the unalterable Good News and we find them all in that one seminal chapter. In Paul's phrase, this is how we set about "testifying to the gospel of the grace of God" (Acts 20 : 24) bearing witness that "the Father sent the Son to be the Saviour of the world" (1 John 4 : 14). This message never changes. It is the unchanging duty of the church—and particularly the church's ministers—to proclaim it. Luther expressed it in those memorable words of the ninety-five Theses—"The true treasure of the church is the most holy Gospel of the glory and the grace of God". That proclamation is the only thing ultimately which we have to offer to sinful men and women of our own or of any other generation.

It is the glory of our Reformation and Evangelical tradition that we concentrate upon this stance and assert its centrality. The minister is but a mouthpiece. His models are the prophets of the Old Testament and John the Baptist, who simply announced the word of the Lord and themselves retired into the background. Thus in our Bible study as believers we concentrate upon the central message. In our church history we look carefully to see *what* was being preached at any particular time. Was it the New Testament gospel? Was it the message of justification by grace alone, through faith in Jesus Christ alone? If that is absent, the church is tottering. When we study our pulpit oratory we delight most of all to read the sermons of the men whose work God has blessed to see just what they were saying. How was it that Whitefield, Edwards, Spurgeon and others were blessed so signally? We rightly attribute this to their loyalty to the unchanging message. The gospel is the *power* of God unto salvation to everyone who believes in Jesus Christ (Rom. 1 : 16).

Yet if this is *all* we "see" in Holy Scripture and in church history, we fall somewhat short of the whole counsel of God. We are missing the rich totality implicit in the reformation call to see all life in the light of God's Word and to live it to his glory. We are falling short of acknowledging that strand in scriptural teaching which lays particular obligations on particular men and societies. We are failing to notice the background of individuals both in Scripture and in church history—their age, their particular psychology, their home, their social standing and other aspects of their setting. The whole counsel of God includes even more than the glorious message of salvation by grace alone, though perhaps everything is in that gospel in embryo.

Revelation includes truths about God himself, about creation, about His law, about the infection of sin which is the breaking of his law, about how he dealt with a nation, about even the nature of history itself which is under his sovereign control. There is this vast backcloth to the gospel, and if our message is not thought out and presented in terms of this backcloth, then the conceptual currency of the gospel—the meaning of the very words we use—is devalued. Transgression, responsibility, merit and grace, judgement and justification itself—all these things lose their point, their colour, their purpose and their impact outside their scriptural context. They are only valid and strong in this total perspective, which our heritage of biblical theology enables us to see clearly.

The context in which Christians live and witness and preach their message is therefore of great importance in another sense. The obligation of contemporary evangelism forces questions upon us. More precisely, who is it speaking the message? And to whom and in what circumstances? What can hinder or facilitate our proclamation? We may sometimes ignore such cultural questions, but they can be crucial. Missionary work, for example, is typically cross-cultural. A messenger from culture A goes to another group in culture B somewhere else and starts preaching and teaching them. It may be the Englishman in Borneo or the North American in Brazil. At once they face cultural problems. They have first to master a language, something which is given by a sovereign God, but an unknown tongue all the same. A new skill has to be acquired in order to communicate anything at all. As men and women are converted and the church begins to grow, they have to scrutinize the surrounding culture and help their converts to understand it and to evaluate it. The missionary is obliged to instruct new Christians how they should live the Christian life in this (to him) totally different environment. Scripture, Spirit-given insight and pastoral teaching will help them to see which factors in their own culture are sinful, which are good and which perhaps are neutral. In a pluralistic and swiftly changing society we do not have to travel overseas to discover similar situations and challenges ourselves within our own country.

So wherever the gospel goes there is the social and human context which is judged and purified at some points, but enriched and approved at other points. To enable this discernment is the work of the Holy Spirit the purifier through the church and through the Word of God. Wherever men of God have gone there have been changes. We are not specifically told that Egypt was better for the presence of Joseph (though this was certainly true economically when the years of famine came!), but it must surely have been better in many ways thanks to a prime minister from the children of Abraham. Babylon had great benefit from the presence of Daniel, Nineveh from the presence of Jonah. The whole culture profits from a faithful testimony to God's Word.

It is not simply that there are converts and heaven rejoices with the church as she grows. When the gospel prospers something else is given to a nation besides individual believers. The whole quality of social life is changed as more and more people apply the Word of God to their own life in the community. In this respect many of us are glad to point out to our doubting friends that seventeenth century England was in many ways a better society after the Reformers and the Puritans, eighteenth century England a healthier place thanks to Whitefield and Wesley, nineteenth century England ennobled by the work of Spurgeon and the others.

Christian testimony, then, is first and foremost to an unchanging gospel. But secondly God's Word is addressed to the particular problems and blessings, vices and privileges, blindness and insights of the age in which the message is being preached. A genuine, full-orbed Christianity insists that everything must be seen in the light of the Holy Spirit and all aspects of life evaluated and lived to the glory of God.

Culture

First a definition. What are we to make of this loosely used word "culture"? The anthropologists tell us that culture is "all learned human behaviour which is socially acquired". In a sense culture is an abstraction. Scholars sometimes divide it into material objects, social institutions, religious practices, linguistic and aesthetic aspects. A related formulation is that which sees culture as a way of behaving, thinking and reacting belonging to a particular group. It is a pattern in which objects and actions become socially and individually meaningful. A fuller definition might be something like this:

Culture is a persisting pattern of thinking, feeling, believing and evaluating, socially acquired by learning as distinct from biologically inherited, through which the cumulative heritage and value systems of a society are transmitted, and by virtue of which both individual meanings and social institutions cohere and continue.

Culture is man-made and all-pervasive. A culture needs careful cherishing, renewal and transmission. Its permanence cannot be taken for granted. It is rich but delicate. It is the essential part of the fabric of human social existence. Without a culture, the human infant develops into nothing more than an animal, as the occasional "wolf-child" has shown.

Now what is the Christian significance of culture? This we must discover in the light of the Word of God and in particular of the early chapters of Genesis. There we see man freely exercising the choice given him by God. Man is not genetically or biologically bound to particular ways of behaving like animals and plants, but free in a profound sense, reflecting God's image. The theology of Genesis embraces the emergence of culture. There are at least three aspects of this which stand out.

(i) *Man is creative:* this is the first and perhaps the deepest aspect. The cultural mandate given to man in Genesis 1 : 28 and 2 : 15, though spoken of primarily in terms of the earth and natural things, clearly extends further to all the ways in which man moulds his environment and the world in which God has placed him. He is to subdue, to have dominion, to till the ground and so on. He is the agent of innovation and change. Though given in an agricultural background, these commands clearly open up all the great extensions of knowledge and control that science and technology and scholarship of all sorts have given us ever since. Man is to adapt the world to his needs, yet he must treat its given structures and delicate balances with respect. He is a steward under God, free but responsible. This emphasises man's main difference from all other parts of the natural order. He *makes* things, tools and weapons, ships, trains and aeroplanes, paintings and temples, cities and factories, music, mathematics and literature.

(ii) *Man has been given rationality:* this is implicit when speech and language become the prominent features of the Genesis narrative. It is interesting to note that God brought the creatures to man to see what he would call them (Gen. 2 : 19). He was not handed language ready-made; he created language for himself. In this he is like his Maker, who *spoke* before man ever existed. Language orders, arranges and clarifies. By it we communicate. Through its use God and man can converse together. By it we argue, persuade, deduce and reason. In that supremely rational skill lies the genesis of all logic, science, philosophy and every symbolic system, mathematics and the arts and so on.

(iii) *Man is moral:* he was under a moral obligation from the time of his creation. The command was apparently a single, simple one, yet he was to live under it. "Thou shalt not eat of it" (Gen. 2 : 17). The story of the Fall shows how disobedience resulted in shattered relationships. Man's communion with his Maker, and with the woman given to him as helper and companion, and with nature around him, were all disjointed and ruined. For this reason everything in human experience since has had to be subject to moral evaluation. The finest achievements are good, *but.* . . . Everywhere there is a strange mixture of comedy and tragedy, of perfection tainted, of nobility flawed. That is why moral approval and disapproval are appropriate to the whole range of human activities. There is a basic moral ambiguity in all things and always has been since the Fall. This is why moral distinctions and mixed reactions are characteristically Christian responses as we study the cultural achievements of mankind.

The culture that man has created is not one in all times and places. We need to use the plural and to speak of "cultures". The anthropologist is keen to tell us of the differences between different cultures over the centuries and in different regions. Through failure to recognise this missionaries and travellers have made many mistakes, some of them humorous, some of them tragic. Whatever may have been the characteristics of the very earliest period, the various cultures of man have very different histories. Geography has had a formative influence in this variety, and there are now identifiable national and racial characteristics. The Christian must consider this variety from a scriptural point of view. All is part of the divine will. Genesis 10 and 11 are in some ways difficult chapters to interpret, but they are certainly telling us at least two things. Firstly, between the Flood and the call of Abraham the human race became diverse, so that as man spread, historical and geographical features differentiated various tribes and nations. Secondly we learn that this variety is somehow both a judgement from God but also a potential source of blessing. Consider the confusion of tongues mentioned in the Babel narrative. This has brought us a barrier between nations, but also the enrichment of a tremendous wealth of contrasting achievement in the great literatures of the world.

Since God has dealt with mankind in this way, in our thinking we have to hold unity and diversity together. This point is taken up by the Apostle Paul in his speech at Athens (Acts 20 : 25) where he speaks of man having been made of one stock, while also stressing at the same time that God had decreed historical and geographical differences, times and places of habitation. So there is a willed diversity, not only of peoples but also of the cultures they produce and which characterise their various national identities. The chosen nation herself, Israel, was given a specific cultural character which she has never completely lost.

Each culture is a source of meaning and continuity to the group to which it belongs. It is a principle of life, coherence and stability. Culture makes myriads of small actions meaningful. Take any item in our own culture. If I advance towards you with my hand out I am a friend—that is a sign, it doesn't need to be explained. In both our minds it bears a cultural significance. One can conceive (and in fact space fiction stories have sometimes been built on the possibility) that to do this to a being from another planet might signify something quite different, and could lead to some great disaster. It is culture, therefore, that gives society its principles of interpretation of behaviour, its codes and roles, its distinctions and enduring character.

But these principles and patterns can be eaten away. The whole shared structure of thought and feeling of a society can disintegrate. The resulting condition is dangerous and can prove disastrous. Such a collapse is something that we in Britain have never experienced in its totality for centuries, but we are beginning to see signs of such a critical event. If a group of people living in the same region have no shared assumptions or shared expectations, a frightening insecurity spreads very quickly. You don't know what the next man means when he says something—you don't know how your neighbour or colleague will react when you face him with a disappointment or a frustration. Suspicion, envy, hatred and alienation begin to take over. Equally serious is the fact that under these conditions there can be no agreement on how to educate our children. There will be insoluble problems for parents and for schools. Eventually we will be faced with anarchy, when every man does that which is right in his own eyes (to use those awful words of that last verse of the Book of Judges), and every man's hand is against his neighbour. Many great civilisations, after reaching tremendous peaks of achievement and social organisation, have disintegrated through loss of inner vision, moral energy, inner coherence. Their cultures have crumbled and passed away. Spengler, the remarkably prophetic German writer of the early years of this century, spent years studying this kind of thing and finally wrote his two volume book, *The Decline of the West* (1918 & 1922). More recently Arnold Toynbee's *Study of History* (1934–1961) has tried to do something similar, enquiring why cultures rise and fall. Both these learned historians chronicle the fact that cultures can and do collapse, and whenever this happens immense suffering is involved. Cultural collapse is not just a concept for academics, a speculative idea for those people who like to think about these things. It is a most ghastly calamity. It is a cruel experience, from which we should be praying that God will deliver us. It is a "fiery trial" for any nation or any church to endure.

Scripture and Culture

A genuine Christianity will, as we have mentioned earlier, constantly assert that *God's Word judges every culture*. Wherever there are God's people, enlightened by his truth and his Word, there is an implicit challenge to contemporary culture. When a man begins to live by the Word of God, and to think and judge by the Word of God, immediately he begins to feel the inadequacies of the culture around him. False suggestions are exposed: evil and ugliness are illuminated. This is effected by a spiritual discernment based upon the revealed law of God. That re-publication of God's character and will, so clearly inspired by the Holy Ghost and set down for us in Scripture, reminds us of what the conscience of man since the Fall has only dimly sensed. Principles emerge from Scripture very clearly to guide us. The priorities of the moral law are clear and inescapable. First, the love and worship of God, and then the love of our neighbour; the sanctity of life and of the family and of my neighbour's goods and of the pledged word. All these things are the common property of Old and New Testament prophets and apostles, assumed and embedded in preaching to the Gentiles and to the Jews alike. These obligations in the conscience of fallen man are all too easily obscured and twisted, but they lie deep in human nature. Since they are now clearly re-published in the Word of God, his people in every age possess a yardstick by which to judge their own culture.

By the light of revelation and by applying God's Word, *certain values in any culture can be welcomed*. Scripture affirms some values in every culture. Wherever man has by grace followed his deepest instincts, there the Christian will find some things of which he can approve. There has never been a culture which has been totally and utterly devoid of the light of conscience. Telling

11

the truth, the search for justice, the approval of compassion, the counselling of self-restraint—wherever we find these things, the Christian will approve of them. Goodness persists, and this means that the Christian and the church of Christ are never totally alienated from the forms of human life which surround them. Peter had to admit the continuation of human goodness and aspiration to high ideals outside the sphere of God's chosen people entrusted with revealed truth when faced with Cornelius (Acts 10 : 35) and Paul made the same kind of guarded admission to the Athenians (Acts 17 : 27–29). The "common grace" of God (as the theologians call it) is found at work in many places. We need, too, to remember the key passage in the second chapter of Paul's Epistle to the Romans (Romans 2 : 1–16). The heathen will all be judged one day because they have sufficient moral discrimination to know what they ought to have done, and that they are transgressors of God's law. On occasion, however, they "do by nature what the law requires . . . though they do not have the law. . . . They show that what the law requires is written on their hearts" (vv. 14–15). To be religiously adrift is not necessarily to be completely morally corrupt. God in his mercy rarely (if ever) allows sin to un-man humanity completely, to de-humanise a person to the ultimate extent, to reduce men to the level of beasts. His grace is secretly at work restraining corruption, keeping the moral sense alive, and we thank God for it. In the light of revelation we discover aspects of every culture where goodness is found, and which Christians can affirm.

We must now add that *the people of God rightly partake of their own culture*, although within the limits set by God's commands. Scriptural characters did this. Besides the example of Joseph in earlier days, we are reminded of Moses in Egypt, who is specifically said to have enjoyed an Egyptian education so that he was skilled in all the wisdom of the Egyptians (Acts 7 : 22). This he did not regret nor was he told to repent of it. Daniel was brought up in Babylon and proved a blessing to his own people and to the nation among whom he lived. Many others have likewise shared the language, the learning, the customs and the dress of those around them, except where the law of God said "no". Where God's commands are clear, his servants have no choice—this far and no further. A culture must not lead us into disobedience. Sometimes we must stand out. Daniel and his friends were unyielding about the food laws (Dan. 1 : 8) and about prayer

(Dan. 3 : 18), despite their privileged position and high political responsibility.

There is nothing sinful about belonging to a particular culture. Scripture itself bears the mark of many cultures. The poetry of Job and the Psalms are outstanding literary achievements. The legislative form of much of the Old Testament regulations in the Pentateuch has a particular near Eastern background and character. The aphorisms of Proverbs and Ecclesiastes can be similarly situated. The historical treatment of Chronicles, Kings and Samuel are of one particular narrative genre, as is the torrential imagery of the Book of Revelation. All these follow forms which are quarried from contemporary culture, taken up as truth by men "moved by the Holy Spirit" (2 Peter 1 : 21), purged of human error.

The lives of the great Christians show that God's greatest servants have also borne the marks of their contemporary culture, and without feeling ashamed. Calvin, for example, was essentially a French renaissance humanist before he was a reformer, and he retained these qualities; they were sanctified to the service of the gospel and the blessing of the church when they were brought into subjection to the Word of God. But Calvin never ceased to be *that* kind of man with *that* kind of training. He displayed those particular gifts nurtured in that kind of culture. Luther was a German to his fingertips and he never ceased to rejoice in that fact—witness his *Table Talk*, and many other works. Incidentally he almost fashioned the German language single-handed by a superb feat of linguistic sensitivity and genius when he translated the Bible. Germany in his time was a mixture of many different dialects; Luther in his Bible translation work took words from many sources. He spent time consulting servant boys and grooms, shepherds and soldiers, travelling ambassadors, dukes and princes, to find out the full range of words current in Germany before he decided which he would use. By this inspired selection he virtually created modern German, and he rejoiced in his German nationality. John Knox was certainly a Scotsman to his dying day, and C. H. Spurgeon was a Victorian Englishman through and through, as well as being one of the greatest preachers of all time. So God's good gifts in and through any culture can not only be *identified* by the man with a Bible in his hand, but they can be properly *enjoyed* by the Christian man. We can take and savour with thankfulness what God gives us through our

13

own particular cultural scene. Human institutions are culturally mediated, and are innocent until they are proved guilty! The Apostle Paul makes the same point (in the context it applies particularly to marriage and food) in 1 Timothy 4 : 4, where we are told that everything that God has created and given by the created order may be received with thankfulness and prayer.

We may go a stage further. *Particular cultural allegiances are permissible for God's people.* Every man and woman belongs to a particular time and place. We develop—and we need—a sense of belonging. To belong to a culture and to rejoice in it and thank God for it is both natural and right. Ultimately Christians must regard cultural factors as provisional: they do not have an absolute claim on us. They are temporary, since we have here no continuing city (Heb. 13 : 14). Though we do not take cultural factors with ultimate seriousness, there is still a place for national and local characteristics, both in individuals and in Churches. The Christian does not need to condemn all forms of national and local patriotism. There can be a healthy corporate pride in the moral or political or artistic or scientific contributions which our particular culture may have made.

It is worth remarking how the need for local allegiances, which is denied by the dreary monochrome of so much of our standardised existence in modern bureaucratic industrial society, is today expressed in the colourful world of sport, and particularly of supporters' clubs. To be a football "fan", for example, may in one sense be part of discovering one's local identity. The Christian supporter will need to be on guard against fanaticism, blind partisanship and the other risks that any kind of mass activity bring with them. But neither he nor his children need be denied these experiences in principle, any more than one would condemn a Christian for his Yorkshire accent. We all put down roots. We all need to know where we belong in space and time. The demand for political devolution in the United Kingdom is not a logical necessity; cultural diversity between regions can co-exist within an area governed by one central power. But where the centre lacks character or integrity or moral conviction and fails to respond to the deepest human needs of the governed population, demands for devolution are only to be expected. Those governments which neglect moral, religious and cultural roots have only themselves to blame. The point we are making here is that various community loyalties and responsibilities have a rightful place in the life of the Christian.

There will therefore be a culture where the Christian is at home, a culture which he feels he understands. It will be a culture which he must set in the light of God's Word, but one which he can love and be thankful for in everything that is good, pure and true. Because a man is a Christian he does not cease to be a man of a particular nation, environment and historical situation.

Our Collapsing Culture

For centuries Western Europe has seen the developing story of Christian civilisation. Behind the varying national and geographical differences lay a common intellectual and moral (even metaphysical) framework. The roots of modern western culture are threefold: the questioning of the Greeks; the organisation and sense of law of the Romans, and thirdly (and most important) the Judaeo-Christian religious and moral contribution. This last influence has been the deepest formative principle in the development of Western European culture. It was this that brought us the dignity of woman, the sacredness of the family, the intellectual base for the rise of modern science, our hospitals, our schools, our universities and—if we are to believe even some of the non-Christian economists—our great economic take-off after the Reformation.

Now the heart of this unique Jewish and Christian view is the concept of man as responsible to some good and just being beyond and outside of himself. One day all men will be judged—such is their dignity and their destiny. Man is accountable and he is under law. This is a basic biblical assumption which Christianity affirmed. The Greeks and the Romans had glimpsed it and groped for it. We are not ignorant of goodness. There is a kind of life we ought to live, and we know it. Christianity affirmed all this with complete clarity through its vision of the positive goodness of a pure and holy God, whose life was lived out on earth through his Son. Through that perfect life and death we are both condemned and saved. Following that unique pattern, Christian values have been built into our laws and our institutions over the centuries.

Millions have profited from the Christian culture of Western Europe who have had no personal faith. Millions have been saved from cruelty, exploitation, degradation, and from other forms of evil simply because the surrounding culture, though imperfect, was one which the gospel had touched. Some of our social pioneers were men and women who had no faith, yet Christian charity and compassion, Christian philanthropy, stress on truth and responsibility and justice were in their bones, and in the light of these ideals they rescued their fellows from exploitation and depravity. In this country we rejoice in a Christian inheritance shaped by the Protestant Reformation, whose theology is that of catholic Christianity in its purest and most glorious form. It is remarkable that when people without any religious convictions are taken from this country quite suddenly and find themselves as teachers, or technologists in some other part of the world, they are forced to ask themselves what is different about Britain, and what has made it the kind of place which is so different. This is a cultural question, but it leads to deeper questions than those about "culture shock". In more than one case it has led men to faith in Jesus Christ.

But Western European culture is now collapsing. Many writers have been studying this disintegration recently—Dr. Schaeffer from his particular point of view in *The God Who is There* (Hodder, 1968) and other books. We had warnings in the 30's and the 40's from one or two prophetic voices, particularly under the stress of the war. Two outstanding works were *The Idea of a Christian Society* (Faber, 1939) by the distinguished Anglo-American poet T. S. Eliot, and the Riddell Lectures by the famous Scottish Presbyterian John Baillie, *What is Christian Civilisation?* (O.U.P. 1945). How much further the decline has gone since then is chronicled by two modern books by evangelical writers of the 1970's—Rookmaaker's *Modern Art and the Death of a Culture* (I.V.P. 1970) and Os Guinness's *Dust of Death* (I.V.P. 1973).

As alienation, hatred and abrasiveness increase daily, our culture seems to be disintegrating. The roots of the disease are clear to thoughtful Christians. The most radical fault dates back a century—it is the lack of the fire and the vision of the gospel. Christianity in Britain has experienced a disastrous decline in the preaching and teaching of the Word of God. The church is weak, and the prevalent religious liberalism prevents her from preaching and expounding God's law. Without the law there is no understanding of the urgency and the glory of the New Testament gospel. There has been no great spiritual revival, though we pray for it. Severed from its health-giving roots, our culture is in swift decline.

No value system is emerging which has a hope of replacing the Christian one. Nothing which any politician or philosopher has to offer the nation can replace the Christian roots of our own culture. Once the Christian vision is rejected there is no core of common allegiances for the people of these islands, no set of standards which they can adhere to and which we can commend as common property. The result of this dangerous vacuum we see in front of us daily in our newspapers. There is constant social friction and increasing bitterness. If things go on as they are and God does not send us revival the outlook is indeed grim.

This disintegration can be evaluated by the Christian in a number of ways. Take the eighteenth chapter of the book of Leviticus, which is part of the Mosaic legislation. It is a frightening study to go through that chapter and ask "How is this word of God judging our culture today?" Those things prohibited to the Israelites as abominations, things which were not even to be named or considered amongst them are all back with us. Behaviour which Western Europe (apart from a few notorious strands in decadent Romanticism) has scarcely seen or thought about as possible for centuries is now made public daily in our paperbacks and newspapers. The chapter in Leviticus begins with incest, recently a theme for more than one popular play on the London stage. It continues with adultery—and everyone knows what is happening to marriage; divorce figures rise every year. Wifeswapping habits and other vicious indecencies are now commended in magazines which you can pick up from any bookstall. Leviticus continues with child murder (v. 21). Most of us know what money is made today out of the abortion racket, to which I shall refer later. Infant bodies are burned in Britain today as surely as they were burned to Molech among the Ammonites of old. The chapter goes on to mention homosexuality, behaviour which is now openly propagated in magazines, and approved or at least tolerated by an increasing group of men in a number of churches. The National Union of Students voted £20,000 in 1973 for the establishment of homosexual clubs in universities and colleges; the news scarcely even made a headline. Leviticus goes on to forbid sexual intercourse between humans and animals—things which can now be seen on the cinema screen in New York and Denmark, and can be found in magazines available in this country. These are the enormities that are with us, every one of them forbidden in that one chapter—the eighteenth chapter of

Leviticus. They pollute a whole community and the very region where they are prevalent—"the land is defiled" (v. 25).

Consider just one of these areas of prohibited conduct. Any man of God with his Bible open will view with the utmost seriousness the eighteenth and nineteenth chapters of Genesis, which record the destruction of Sodom. He will also note that the first chapter of the Epistle to the Romans condemns the sin of sodomy in a particular terrifying way. We are not speaking here of tendencies or temptations. These are not sin in themselves. All the children of Adam are mentally and emotionally attracted to conduct which breaks God's laws. This attraction can and must be resisted. What Scripture condemns is the deliberate satisfaction of homosexual desire in forbidden behaviour— sodomy. Homosexual practices are against nature and against revealed truth. They are not simply something which ought to fill us with revulsion. Homosexual indulgence is something which God condemns as the ultimate sign of decadence and degradation in any culture. It is made abundantly clear both from the way Sodom is spoken of in Genesis, and from the way Paul writes, that this is a general cultural judgement. It is not purely a transgression by the individual sinner, but the degradation of a whole society. If this vice becomes tolerated and commonplace, as appears to be the case today in Britain, we are very near the end of the road. So from this alone I would deduce that we are approaching the last stages of the disintegration of our culture. For we bear the mark of the lowest decadence of all.

Christians are called upon to *feel* this depressing condition. Quite naturally, if we partake in our own culture, if it is *our* culture we see disintegrating and straying far from the Word of God, we cannot but be deeply conscious of this desperate situation. There will be a sense of loss. It is like being in a house that is steadily being pulled down around you. But we shall also feel it because we know that divinely given structures are being pulled down. It is not just that our culture is being destroyed. Those very things which God in his mercy has set up to restrain sin are being systematically torn down. God is being defied in a land which he has specially blessed in the past.

This consciousness can bite very deep into the Christian heart. I have always been very moved by these words which I read in a church history book: "on the 24th August in the Year of the City 1164, and in the year of our Lord Jesus Christ 410, the Goths

18

under Alaric entered and sacked Rome. 'My voice sticks in my throat', says Jerome, 'and sobs choke me as I dictate. The city which took the whole world captive is itself taken'. Jerome uttered the sensations of all, both Christian and heathen. There has been no such shock to Europe since." So wrote Charles Williams in *The Descent of the Dove*. (We do well to remember that the last sentence was written in 1939 before we opened the doors of Belsen, Dachau and Buchenwald). The sack of Rome sent a tremor throughout Christianity; Jerome's words show a Christian feeling deeply the collapse of a culture. I believe he was right to feel it as he did.

There is yet another reason why the Christian cannot but feel distress. As a culture collapses people get hurt. If my love for my neighbour means anything to me at all, the fact that my neighbour and my neighbour's children are now open to subtle forms of media-controlled, psychologically-dominated poison must surely make me feel sorrow and compassion for them. Christians are called upon to sympathise—and compassion and sympathy mean "to suffer with". In addition, our grief will be even greater where the culture is a largely Christian one, fashioned and formed and guided over centuries by the principles of revealed morality. Our own culture has had the gospel, the Bible and influence of the church. Today we watch professional ethics, which often embody Christian values, being ditched without a thought week by week. One has only to consider doctors and nurses. Who would have thought five years ago of a nurses' strike or a consultants' strike? Now we take them for granted. We have watched the erosion of the Lord's Day, the ousting of the Bible from the schools, the rescinding of legislation which restrained witchcraft, blasphemy, homosexuality, abortion and stage obscenity. All these things the Christian should feel deeply. An earlier writer gave good advice when he wrote in an exposition of the Beatitudes:

Mourn for the errors and blasphemies of the nation. There is now a free trade of error. Toleration gives men a patent to sin. What cursed opinion that has been long ago buried in the Church but is now digged out of the grave and by some worshipped? Mourn for covenant violation. This sin is a flying roll against England. Breach of covenant is spiritual harlotry and for this God may name us "Lo-ammi" and give us a bill of divorce. Mourn for the pride of the nation; our condition is low but our hearts are high. Mourn for the profaneness of the land: England is like that man in the Gospel who had a spirit of an unclean devil. Mourn for the removing of landmarks. Mourn for the contempt offered to the magistracy: the spitting in the face of authority. Mourn that there are so few mourners. Surely if we mourn not for the sins of others it is to be feared we are not sensible of our own sins. God looks down upon us as guilty of those sins in others which we do not lament. Our tears may help us to quench God's wrath.

So wrote Thomas Watson in 1660.

Our Response

In these apparently terminal stages of our culture, what should be our Christian response? We shall sketch in this section the theological position which is the only firm basis.

Firstly we must avoid *Christian insulation*. I think this is implicit in much of what has already been said. The desire to be a hermit or to enter the monastery is not one which belongs solely to the Roman tradition. There is a "little flock" mentality which has always been very congenial to many Evangelicals. Such a feeling, noble in its way, was one of the factors that led the Brethren ("Plymouth Brethren") to leave the Church of England in the last century, and that still lead many into small protected enclaves. So much of our contemporary culture has the smell of the pit upon it that dedicated Christians find this withdrawal a great temptation. If we do not discover something of that within us we may have to doubt our own spirituality, because it is the first and most natural reaction to want to get away from it all. What a delight it is to be together with Christian brothers and sisters. How we long to seek for a place of communion with God, for fellowship, for a place where at least we can encourage each other in what we know to be right and good and to live according to the will of our Father. This response is a natural one for earnest and sensitive Christians, and there are even verses in Scripture which, taken by themselves, might suggest that this is right. It is indeed our duty to keep ourselves unspotted from the world, to have no fellowship with the unfruitful works of darkness (James 1 : 27, Eph. 5 : 11) and so on. Yet this withdrawal is no real option for the Christian, since as well as keeping himself unspotted from the world, he has to "visit the fatherless and the widows in their affliction." Compassionate, comforting, outgoing ministry is demanded of us wherever there is need. Not only are we to have no fellowship with the unfruitful works of darkness but we have a ministry of exposing them (Eph. 5 : 11), reproving and rebuking. This means knowing about them. It means remaining in the world in order that we may know what is going on in it and help and save others. Perhaps the best-known verse of all is the command of Jesus to His followers to be "the salt of the earth". Salt is the traditional preservative which has to be rubbed in. It cannot stay separate and apart if it is to preserve. Jesus prayed that his disciples should not be taken out of the world, but that his Father would "keep them from the evil one" (John 17 : 15).

Christians in the reformation tradition must avoid "out-calvining Calvin"! This is always our temptation when we greatly admire a man of God. The Calvinistic doctrine of original sin and total depravity when taken in its scriptural sense is right and proper. Sin has indeed infected every human being and every human activity to some degree. But such assertions can lead to some very subtle perversions of the Christian's attitude to the world. We can be persuaded to talk about "a sick society", "a corrupt country", "a morally decadent community" and so on. These are phrases which we hear on other people's lips; the Marxist, for example, loves to say this kind of thing too. We can be making statements which are true, yet they can lead others into error or confusion. We can sit and shake our heads in a satisfied way, saying "I told you so. This is what was bound to happen. Some of us have been saying it for many years." We can look at our humanist friends and we can say "Your efforts are getting you nowhere, you have got no answer, have you? Look at the way things are getting worse." There can be a kind of rejoicing about the way that we say it. Evangelicals can turn to the advocates of a liberal theology, or Calvinists to their Arminian friends, and say "You have no adequate diagnosis of this situation, have you?" It is true, of course, they haven't. It is also true that—by the grace of God—the believer armed with reformation theology is fully equipped. But we can also take a kind of delight in every evil thing which proves our case, and this is wrong. Love "hopeth all things" (1 Cor. 13 : 7). Delight in evil is always wrong. Such is not the reaction of the true Christian man, and it certainly cannot be attributed to Calvin. But it is in practice an easy step from the scriptural teaching on man's depravity as expressed, for example, in the Westminster Confession. There are Christians whose orthodoxy is beyond question, but who have been caught by this attitude: "What better can you expect of sinful man?" Then they sit back and say "I told you so." Perhaps not in so many words, but this is really what it comes to.

Godly men do not respond thus to human confusion and wickedness. It is not the reaction of God's prophets in the Old Testament, nor is it the reaction of our Lord over Jerusalem. Who ever had better justification for saying "I told you so" than he did? Yet he did it with weeping and with tears. It is high time some of us recalled Knox's agony over Scotland or Spurgeon's grief over London. The man of God is involved, not insulated. We are not meant to be scurrying away to our burrows of intellectual and theological impregnability where we can safely deplore the continuing corruption.

Where is the compassion for our neighbours who risk being overwhelmed in the disaster? Where is the confidence in a sovereign God among those huddled behind their defences? Our Lord Jesus Christ has not been pushed off the throne. He reigns, invested with all authority. There must be no talk of the ghetto and no talk of retreat. We must condemn a spiritual sleight-of-hand which turns good theology into an excuse for doing nothing. The New Testament never argues from original sin to Christian gloom and passivity. Obviously we need our fellowship and our teaching and our meetings for prayer, but only in order to go on afterwards and to grapple with the hosts of Satan and storm the strongholds of evil in church and community.

This introduces us to a pressing obligation. There is a positive task—to *revive the concept of active Christian citizenship*, which has almost died over the last hundred years. It was there in Victorian England, particularly towards the beginning of the century. Yet in the second half of the nineteenth century it gradually died. It must be revived. Here is an urgent teaching ministry for today, if ever there was one. We can approach this on the lowest level possible first, that of sheer opportunity. We live in a democracy, which means that every man's and woman's voice counts. We have a vote locally and a vote nationally. We can write letters which have a chance of being printed, we can make ourselves heard in all sorts of ways. If we lived in the Soviet Union or in any of the other Marxist states, then perhaps the little Christian ghetto in the back room might be the only thing we could fashion and influence. The Lord would not judge us for that. But in fact we still live in a land which has a form of democracy. We still inhabit a country in which our voice for goodness and purity and justice can be heard. We can make our presence felt. Is this not, therefore, an open door? Are we not under a clear obligation to participate and to use our voice for the standards which we know God has revealed?

Now there are two scriptural pillars to Christian citizenship—the doctrine of the state and the doctrine of Law. The place of the state is outlined in Romans 13. The state has a moral value and an ethical function, not simply because it prevents anarchy, but also because it is God who speaks through this institution of sinful man. There are, of course, limits to what the state can tell us to do. The state is never infallible. Scripture makes these limits plain, too. Because government is God's ordinance and the voice of God may be heard in human legislation and in the exercise of earthly authority, there is no barrier whatsoever which prevents Christians from taking part in the legislative process or in administration right up to the highest level. Now search your parliamentary guides for your unashamedly Christian MP's whose conscience is "captive to the Word of God" (to use Luther's memorable phrase), comb your local council chambers for an evangelical local councillor, look at your list of magistrates and ask yourself how many you know (or have heard of) who are Christian people! Those who *are* there have great opportunities. I am sure that defective theology has kept many from such positions of responsibility.

The doctrine of Law is the other pillar. The moral law of God, so the Reformers taught, had a threefold function. Firstly it restrained sin and preserved order; secondly it brought home to a man that he was personally responsible for his conduct, and above all, to God, and thus created conviction of sin, and thirdly it guided the Christian in his conduct. Now this rich and productive understanding of the threefold function of divine law is our Reformation heritage. In the 1940's a well-known liberal theologian, Dr. Alec Vidler, rediscovered this and was so impressed that he wrote a book about it. It didn't make him an evangelical, sad to say, but it certainly pulled him up in his tracks and made him a better theologian than he would have been otherwise. He wrote a book called *Christ's Strange Work* (S.C.M. 1944, 2nd edn. 1963) in which, as if it had lain buried for centuries, he simply recorded his rediscovery of what the Reformers had taught about the law. In presenting this threefold use of the law he was saying, in effect: "Isn't this marvellous; isn't this just what we need?" Vidler was right—and even those in the Reformation tradition have not always seen the richness of their heritage. There is much here for the evangelical today to learn again.

These are the twin pillars upon which we must revive the concept of active Christian citizenship. We should note that Sir Fred Catherwood in his excellent little booklet *The Christian in Contemporary Society* and at greater length in his book *The Christian Citizen* has tried to unpack the implications of this theology in the world of the 1970s.

Our Activity

What types of activity might we be expected to engage in as we catch this vision of active Christian citizenship? How might ministers be encouraging and teaching their congregations? Much of the answer has already been implied.

Of first importance is the *use of the Word of God to identify evil.* Not that there is always a text or a doctrine to give a direct answer to every problem. Where we cannot be definite we must be careful. Not all political, economic and social policies have a verse of Scripture to justify them or to condemn them. But there *are* issues in our society, matters of life, death and the family, issues of human dignity and human love, which are absolutely crystal clear from Scripture. There is a given biblical pattern. Thus we can say that murder, abortion, euthanasia are attacks on the value of human life itself. (Though Scripture clearly enjoins the death penalty for murder, and does not come down on one side or the other in the case of the doctor's dilemma when only one life can be saved—pregnant mother or unborn child—a rare situation in which Christians have always acknowledged no clear-cut obligation.) We can look at fornication, prostitution, homosexuality and other perversions and say these defile family life and are contrary to the will of God. We can consider idolatry, blasphemy, obscenity and we can say these degrade what we know to be good and beautiful in religion and in culture. We can look at Sabbath-breaking, exploitation and injustice in the economic world and we can say that these (or things very like them) were condemned from the days of the prophets onwards; they are contrary to the divine pattern for a healthy society. There is much that we can say when we use the Word of God to identify clear-cut evils. We must read, write, preach and teach for a fresh biblical discrimination. What a privilege it is to expound and apply the Old Testament in days like our own!

Second only to the employment of scriptural criteria comes the need to *try to understand the times and channels by which evil is spread*. Cultural corruption spreads moral decay and social disintegration. So we ask ourselves "How is Satan active? How is he getting this grip on our culture, splintering, fragmenting and poisoning it?" It is not difficult to give the main answers. The press, books, and magazines, film and theatre, radio and TV—the media—are paramount. Then at a deeper level we need to study the attacks upon institutions—the family, school and the legal system in the way in which they have traditionally been conceived, largely under Christian influence. All these have been deeply penetrated by Satanic forces in the last two or three decades. We are conscious of a poisoning of the atmosphere of this country, and the scene gets worse daily. If this continues, then darkness will indeed descend. In this general survey there is no opportunity to be more specific. The book list on page 32 suggests titles of works for further reading. We need to study, and avoid making wild judgements or false accusations. But when we have discovered how these things are working, we must expose and oppose them.

Thirdly, we must *never reject alliances*. We can join with others to fight specific issues. Where there are other Christians—even where there are non-Christians—who on a specific issue will denounce a manifest evil and determine to fight it, there we have a platform on which others may make common cause with us. As unashamed Christians we make no apology for our reasons in what we are doing. We tell the others, any audience we address or any group we organise, that we are in this fight because we are the servants of the Lord Jesus Christ. We confess that the law of God, our loving Father, forbids these things; we know that they will only bring cruelty, suffering and chaos. We make no bones about our allegiance, for we are men under authority. Yet at the same time we can say to others, "If you will join with us to fight this we welcome you." There are many who will have us on our own terms in present circumstances. In addition there is sometimes an opportunity for the Gospel itself to come to people who would never hear it except under these "alliance conditions". (That is not the reason why we agree to alliances, of course; our motive is obedience to God. We pray and work for his will to be done on earth as it is in heaven.) Let no one despise those men of goodwill who will join with us on specific issues.

These temporary alliances on moral issues cover many areas of social concern. Advertising, care for the living world, care for the high standards of our cultural heritage in education, opposition to the contraceptive lobby and the abortion racket—on all these things we ought to be joining with others. We join with allies without apology and without concealing our own position. Our position is that wherever there are men who will stand with us we will accept their help in opposing all that is devilish and destructive. Let me give one example. Early in 1975 a remarkable book, *Babies for Burning* appeared. This ghastly record was the result of investigations by two non-Christian reporters who worked for *The News of the World*. These two young journalists started out simply to investigate what was going on in the world of abortion in London. What they found horrified them to such a degree that they wrote a series of articles in *The News of the World* and then produced this book. They went to various places in London which were advertised on tube stations and in newspapers—pregnancy advisory centres. They pretended to be a young couple who had a baby on the way and didn't really want it. Suggestions were made to them by doctors and nurses. In nearly every case they were advised that the best thing to do would be to have this baby destroyed. Every conversation was tape-recorded. Men and women and organisations are named, with addresses too, in this book. Abortion for sheer convenience and for commercial gain is with us on a massive scale. What is going on in this country to human babies is absolutely unspeakable. One baby every four minutes in the 24 hours, 365 days in the year, is being "terminated" in the very place which ought to be the safest place in God's universe for any baby—its mother's womb. Surely this is a cold savagery which calls down the judgement of God upon this country—more than anything else in the land at the moment. There are admittedly other things which are foul and ugly in our national life, but I think this probably takes pride of place in the utter callousness and cruelty of it all.

The one serious effort to discredit the authors has failed. Most of the tape-recorded interviews are still available for inspection by authorised bodies. Ronald Butt, political correspondent of *The Times* wrote three articles on this book in the early months of 1975, but since that date the press, television and radio have been utterly silent. We should ask ourselves why. Where are Christian people who will stand up and say this must be stopped? This is simply one of the things going on in the land today where Christian people ought to be up in arms, allied with every other person of good will who will join us. We ought to refuse to be silenced until we can find out how and why this ghastly trade is being carried on without any effective curb. And where stricter legislation is appropriate—as it certainly is in this case—Christians should support it.

Fourthly, Christian study must not stop at Scripture and contemporary social trends. We must *get to grips with the intellectual debate*. Some of us at least are called to master what may (perhaps rather inaccurately!) be called the "secular arguments". There is a theological rationale to this. Because man is made in God's image, what God forbids will go against the grain of his created human nature. Certain types of behaviour man learns by bitter experience to be harmful and destructive. Man is aware of certain truths from conscience and from history without having the law of God. Christians know how they ought to live from Scripture, and we can say to ourselves and to our children, "We must not go down that road, for that way leads to danger, damage and perhaps destruction." Others have had to find this out by actually travelling that way and suffering the consequences themselves, or by watching their fellow man coming to grief. In a word, there are good arguments from experience, from history and from psychology against certain types of behaviour which Scripture condemns and it is useful for Christian people to know these arguments. It is useful to be able to make a two-fold attack using both the "sword of the Spirit" and the evidence of the psychologist or historian! Then the Christian can assert that our Father in heaven did not forbid us this or that action because he wanted to put something arbitrary in our way. He forbad certain paths to us because if we go down them we are made in such a way that we shall get hurt. The moral prohibitions of the Bible were given in *love*.

Take for example the area of marriage, linked as it is with child development and human relationships. The Russians tried to abolish marriage for a few years after the Revolution. They found that people began to get so disturbed, and in particular the children coming into the world became such burdens on Soviet society, that they brought back the old bourgeois idea of one man and one woman staying together for good. They brought back marriage, in other words. This is the kind of thing that we need to know. Some of us are called to master these arguments from the world of scholarly investigation.

Protestant theology in the Reformation tradition is no stranger to this position. A fine example is the magisterial work of the distinguished Princeton theologian Charles Hodge (1797–1878). In his *Systematic Theology* (1872–3, repr. 1960), he devotes more than 200 pages of his third volume to an exposition of God's law and Christian morality. Hodge on the Ten Commandments offers a rich mine of ethical teaching. The reader discovers that under almost every commandment he amasses the arguments from nature, from conscience, from experience and from history, as well as expounding from the purely scriptural text that this or that action is forbidden for God's people. We find the same approach in a more modern publication—the Longford Report on *Pornography* (1972). It contains contributions from Sir Fred Catherwood, Bishop Trevor Huddleston and others who write from a Christian point of view about man as made in God's image; they employ scriptural arguments which Christians acknowledge. But other chapters are written by people who are not Christians—Peter Grosvenor, David Holbrook and others. Their penetrating observations supply us with valuable ammuni-. tion when we engage in this particular battle or discussion, considerations which, though not dependent upon Scripture, corroborate Scripture's testimony. Man is simply made in such a way that the prescriptions of the pornographers point the way of decadence and corruption.

Fifthly, we need to remember the Christian duty of *strengthening those things that remain* (Rev. 3 : 2). There are still restraints in our society upon evil. Gleams of truth still penetrate in the most unexpected ways. From time to time we find that suddenly somebody writes an article, or publishes a book, or stands up and says something in public which humbles and encourages the Christian. We never thought it could happen. Perhaps a newspaper columnist whom we had completely written off suddenly glimpses something and is bold enough to say it. It can happen in all sorts of ways. Truth and goodness break through the darkness. Whenever it happens we must strengthen those books, those speakers, whose writers who come out for Christian standards. There are good laws passed from time to time. The legislation of the 1960s concerning morals was mostly in the other direction. Whenever law reform is in question we should be active; the abortion debate is a case in point. James White's Abortion Law (Amendment) Bill which came before the Commons recently was largely due to pressure from the Society for the Protection of Unborn Children, helped on by every M.P's. having been sent a copy of the book *Babies for Burning:* many of them have read it, but there is a very strong rearguard action against James White and his friends. Here is one case for Christian action to strengthen a weak law—the 1967 Abortion Act.

Our mandate to strengthen the things that remain stretches right across the cultural scene. Good laws, family integrity according to the scriptural pattern, anything pure and good in culture and in nature, anything which provides a vision of excellence, moral excellence above all, but also beauty in every form—all should have Christian support. Many Christians have not seen their calling to promote and defend the beautiful. What an ugly world we live in in so many ways! Good music and good literature are all part of our precious but fragile heritage. So much modern architecture, design and decoration is devoid of any idea of grace, or delicacy or even human comfort. This is just symptomatic of a culture in deep conflict, unsure of itself, on the edge of anarchy. Incidentally our architects are just becoming conscious that the design of their tower blocks of flats have actually done things to neighbourhood solidarity and to family life. Christians ought to be in the forefront of this kind of consciousness, supporting all kinds of environmental sensitivity, asking and arguing for different types of housing and for protection from the visual desecration of our surroundings.

As Reformation Christians and evangelical believers we know our primary task. In the power of the Holy Ghost we are called to proclaim the gospel of light. But we also stand, very unworthily, in the tradition of Wilberforce, of Shaftesbury, of Josephine Butler and William Booth; nineteenth century Evangelicals who worked on and on and on against tremendous odds and apathy, even against the hostility of the ecclesiastical and political "establishments" of their day, until they got the laws changed, the slaves freed, and the children out of the mines and out of the brothels.

It is possible that our culture may collapse as did the culture of Rome. We know that the church of Jesus Christ will still persist, because we have his promise that the gates of hell cannot prevail against it (Matt. 16 : 18). The church behind the Iron Curtain flourishes despite all that hostile powers can do. But meanwhile it is our responsibility to arrest this decay wherever we can, to fight the pollution that is at present being publicly disseminated into the families of our land, and particularly to our children. We must provide havens of light and goodness to alleviate suffering. This is no unworthy task. It is our bounden duty. It is to this active involvement that God is calling many more Christian men and women in our land today. Not everyone can do everything, and some people can do nothing but pray (which may well turn out to be the most important ministry of all!). But many, many more could be doing far more than they are doing. If every adult Christian man and woman in this land knew just something about some of these fundamental moral issues and the rate at which decadence was advancing, so much could be done. The letters would pour in to MP's, Government ministers, councillors, newspapers and the broadcasting authorities. The agencies fighting moral corruption would get so much more support. Do we really care for people at all if we have no concern for the collapsing culture which surrounds them and fashions their beliefs, attitudes and behaviour? The task of cultural renewal cannot succeed without Christian light and life. Even with Christian involvement it *may* be destined to fail. The outcome is the Lord's not ours to determine.

There is not much time left to reconquer our culture for our Lord Jesus Christ. It is nearly—but not quite—too late. Yet a fatalistic acceptance of doom is no Christian response. Toynbee reminds us that

. . . The malady which holds the children of decadence fast bound in misery and iron is no paralysis of their natural faculties as human beings but a *breakdown and disintegration of their social heritage*, which debars them from finding scope for their unimpaired faculties in effective and creative social action. (*A Study of History*, 1-vol. edn. Oxford, 1972, p. 155. The italics are not in the original.)

Decadence is seen here as a cultural problem, a dislocation of transmission, a failure in teaching, learning and energising. Others may be paralysed, unable to take social action. But who can paralyse the Christian believer living in the power of the Holy Spirit?

The root cause of the moral decline and cultural disintegration of Britain is undoubtedly to be found in the failure of the professing churches to testify to the goodness and severity of God, to the awesome Creator whose holiness convicts us but whose grace provides a wonderful pardon and restoration at the cost of the blood of the Divine Son. Failure to preach and to live by this gospel deprives a society of the preservative "salt" which the church is commanded to become. When the truth of God is adulterated or submerged in the churches, the whole community suffers, so closely is godliness linked with unrighteousness. This is clear from a study of the Apostle's teaching in the first chapter of his Letter to the Romans. Churches deprived of the gospel and the strong meat of biblical doctrine and exhortation become conformed to the world, weak compromisers, at the mercy of every changing trend of intellectual fashion or every doctrinal innovator. Worship becomes either irreverent or irrelevant, since the vision of the only God worthy of worship has disappeared. If the moral and theological confusion of today sends some professing Christians back to the Bible to rediscover their roots in the apostolic testimony (and some *do* find their way back through the morass of modish radicalism to the foundation truths of the New Testament) we can only rejoice. A renewal of the professing church in truth, in love and in power could yet transform the nation. Church leaders of the past 100 years bear a heavy responsibility for their failure to hold the churches on a true course. Church leaders of today have a wonderful opportunity to proclaim fearlessly the faith once delivered to the saints. Then we should see the churches in ferment (the gospel, as Luther so often said, always causes controversy) but nevertheless creative and powerful, as men and women are won to Christ through the proclamation of the old Gospel—which is in fact the only means of renewal and re-creation to every one who believes in every generation.

Yet there is a mute rebuke to many of those who have remained faithful to the apostolic faith of the New Testament. It lies in our Lord's best known parable. The orthodox were so concerned with their religous tasks that they passed by on the other side, while the heretic was the man who saw the wounded traveller and had compassion, went to him and bound up his wounds, pouring in oil and wine, and set him on his beast and brought him to an inn and took care of him.

FOR FURTHER READING

Social, Literary and General

ELIOT, T. S.: *Notes Towards a Definition of Culture* (Faber 1971)

GUMMER, J. S. : *The Permissive Society* (Cassell 1971)

LITCHFIELD, M. and KENTISH, S.: *Babies for Burning* (Serpentine 1974)

Ed. LONGFORD: *Pornography: The Longford Report* (Coronet 1972)

MANNERS, E.: *The Vulnerable Generation* (Cassell 1971)

MCMILLAN, J.: *The Roots of Corruption* (Stacey 1972)

RICHARDS, P. G.: *Parliament and Conscience* (Allen & Unwin 1970)

STEINER, G.: *In Bluebeard's Castle* (Faber 1971)

TOYNBEE, A.: *A Study of History* (1 vol. edn.) (Oxford 1972)

TREVELYAN, J.: *What the Censor Saw* (Michael Joseph 1973)

WILLIAMS, D.: *Trousered Apes* (Churchill 1971)

WILLIAMS, R.: *Culture and Society* (Penguin 1961) (1st edn. 1958)

Theological

BAILLIE, J.: *What is Christian Civilisation?* (OUP 1945)

BRUNNER, E.: *Christianity and Civilisation* (Nisbet 1958)

CAILLET, E.: *The Christian Approach to Culture* (Abingdon (USA) 1953)

CATHERWOOD, H. F. R.: *The Christian Citizen* (Hodder 1969)

CATHERWOOD, H. F. R.: *A Better Way* (IVF 1975)

ELIOT, T. S.: *The Idea of a Christian Society* (Faber 1939)

GUINNESS, O.: *Dust of Death* (IVP 1973)

NIDA, E. A.: *Culture, Customs and Christianity* (Tyndale 1963)

NIEBUHR, E. R.: *Christ and Culture* (New York (USA) 1951)

ROOKMAAKER, H. R.: *Modern Art and the Death of a Culture* (IVP 1970)

TILLICH, P.: *Faith and Culture* (OUP 1959)

VAN TIL, H. R.: *The Calvinistic Concept of Culture* (Baker (USA) 1959)

VIDLER, A.: *Christ's Strange Work* (SCM 1944, 1963)

WILLIAMS;, C.: *The Descent of the Dove* (Religious Book Club (SCM) 1939)